A
FINE
ROMANCE

A FINE ROMANCE

75 YEARS OF ROYAL WEDDINGS

Edited by
Lisette du Plessis

hardie grant books
MELBOURNE · LONDON

in association with PQ Blackwell

PART ONE

75 YEARS OF ROYAL WEDDINGS

A FINE
75 YEARS

3 February 1968
Princess Benedikte of Denmark married Prince Richard zu Sayn-Wittgenstein-Berleburg.

. . . .

20 November 1947
Princess Elizabeth of the United Kingdom married Lieutenant Philip Mountbatten.

19 April 1956
Sovereign Prince Rainier III of Monaco married Grace Patricia Kelly.

6 May 1960
Princess Margaret of the United Kingdom married Antony Armstrong-Jones.

14 May 1962
Prince Juan Carlos of Spain married Princess Sofía of Greece.

10 March 1966
Princess Beatrix of the Netherlands married Claus von Amsberg.

29 August 1968
Crown Prince Harald of Norway married Sonja Haraldsen.

15 June 1974
Princess Christina of Sweden married Tord Magnuson.

19 June 1976
King Carl XVI Gustaf of Sweden married Silvia Renate Sommerlath.

1930s — 1940s — 1950s — 1960s — 1970s

7 January 1937
Princess Juliana of the Netherlands married Prince Bernhard of Lippe-Biesterveld.

. . . .

3 June 1937
Duke Edward of the United Kingdom married Wallis Simpson.

15 May 1953
Princess Ragnhild of Norway married Erling Lorentzen.

2 July 1959
Prince Albert of Belgium married the Italian Princess Paola Ruffo of Calabria.

12 January 1961
Princess Astrid of Norway married Johan Martin Ferner.

. . . .

25 & 30 May 1961
Princess Birgitta of Sweden married Prince Johann Georg of Hohenzollern.

29 April 1964
Princess Irene of the Netherlands married Prince Carlos of Bourbon-Parma.

. . . .

5 June 1964
Princess Désirée of Sweden married Baron Niclas Silfverschiöld.

. . . .

30 June 1964
Princess Margaretha of Sweden married John Ambler.

. . . .

18 September 1964
Princess Anne-Marie of Denmark married King Constantine II of Greece.

10 January 1967
Princess Margriet of the Netherlands married Pieter van Vollenhoven.

. . . .

10 June 1967
Princess Margrethe, Heir Apparent of Denmark, married Count Henri André of Laborde de Monpezat.

14 November 1973
Princess Anne of the United Kingdom married Captain Mark Phillips.

28 June 1975
Princess Christina of the Netherlands married Jorge Guillermo.

28 June 1978
Princess Caroline of Monaco married Philippe Junot.

ROMANCE
OF ROYAL WEDDINGS

17 & 19 May 2001
Prince Constantijn
of the Netherlands
married Laurentien
Brinkhorst.

12 April 2003
Prince Laurent of
Belgium married
Claire Coombs.

....

29 July 1981
Prince Charles
of the United
Kingdom
married Lady
Diana Spencer.

22 September 1984
Princess Astrid of
Belgium married
Arch-Duke Lorenz
d'Autriche-Este.

12 December 1992
Anne, The Princess
Royal, of the United
Kingdom married
Commander
Timothy Laurence.

4 October 1997
Infanta Cristina
of Spain married
Iñaki Urdangarín.

25 August 2001
Crown Prince
Haakon of Norway
married Mette-Marit
Tjessem Høiby.

12 September 2003
Princess Stéphanie
of Monaco married
Adans Lopez Peres.

9 April 2005
Prince Charles
of the United
Kingdom married
Camilla Parker
Bowles.

19 June 2010
Crown Princess
Victoria of
Sweden married
Daniel Westling.

1980s   1990s   2000s   2010s

29 December 1983
Princess Caroline
of Monaco married
Stefano Casiraghi.

23 July 1986
Prince Andrew
of the United
Kingdom married
Sarah Ferguson.

18 March 1995
Infanta Elena of
Spain married Jaime
de Marichalar y
Sáenz de Tejada.

....

1 July 1995
Princess Stephanie
of Monaco married
Daniel Ducruet.

....

18 November 1995
Prince Joachim of
Denmark married
Alexandra
Christina Manley.

23 January 1999
Princess Caroline
of Monaco married
Prince Ernst of
Hanover.

....

19 June 1999
Prince Edward
of the United
Kingdom married
Sophie Rhys-Jones.

....

4 December 1999
Crown Prince
Philippe of Belgium
married Mathilde
d'Udekem d'Acoz.

2 February 2002
Crown Prince
Willem-Alexander
of the Netherlands
married
Máxima Zorreguieta.

....

24 May 2002
Princess Märtha
Louise of Norway
married Ari Mikael
Behn.

24 April 2004
Prince Johan Friso
of the Netherlands
married Mabel
Wisse Smit.

14 May 2004
Crown Prince
Frederik of
Denmark married
Mary Elizabeth
Donaldson.

....

22 May 2004
Prince Felipe of
Spain married
Letizia Ortiz.

24 May 2008
Prince Joachim of
Denmark married
Marie Agathe
Odile Cavallier.

....

29 April 2011
Prince William
of the United
Kingdom married
Catherine
Middleton.

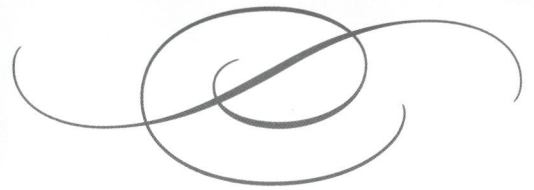

1930s

7 JANUARY 1937

Princess Juliana of the Netherlands (Queen Juliana from 1948–1980) married Prince Bernhard of Lippe-Biesterveld.

3 JUNE 1937

Duke Edward of the United Kingdom (King Edward VIII from January–December 1936) married Wallis Simpson.

3 June 1937, France – Duke Edward of the United Kingdom (King Edward VIII from January–December 1936) married Wallis Simpson at the Chateau de Cande.

"I have found it impossible to carry the
heavy burden of responsibility and to discharge
my duties as King as I would wish to do without
the help and support of the woman I love."

Edward VIII – from broadcast after his abdication, 11 December 1936

DUKE EDWARD • WALLIS SIMPSON

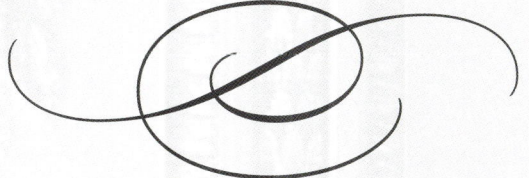

1940s

20 November 1947

Princess Elizabeth of the United Kingdom
(Queen Elizabeth II from 1952–present) and
Lieutenant Philip Mountbatten.

20 November 1947, England – Princess Elizabeth of the United Kingdom (Queen Elizabeth II from 1952–present) married Lieutenant Philip Mountbatten at Westminster Abbey, London.

"Had our purses and our warehouses been fuller, today's celebrations in honour of the marriage of Princess Elizabeth and the Duke of Edinburgh would have been decked in brighter and more costly colours, but not more spontaneous or moving.

The ceremony inside Westminster Abbey has been planned with elegance and wisdom and the bride's own choice of music shows the good taste which might be expected from a Doctor of Music at London University. If only the weather will mend its ways this morning the crowds along the Mall and Whitehall will count the waiting hours of slight account for the momentary glimpse of glass coach and Sovereign's escort in full uniform, of foreign kings and queens, and all the trappings of a state occasion. Many will listen to the broadcast commentaries. The first plan for an austere wedding has been changed in accordance with the wishes of nation and Empire just as, 131 years ago, in times no less worrying, the wedding of Princess Charlotte and Prince Leopold assumed a dignity far exceeding the Prince Regent's early intentions. Someone showed poor understanding of public opinion who in July supposed that because most people today are shabby and constrained with coupons and permits they would prefer the Princess to have a utility wedding. The greyer the general outlook, the keener the popular desire for the glitter of spectacles and the sound of fanfares."

From the *Manchester Guardian*, 20 November 1947

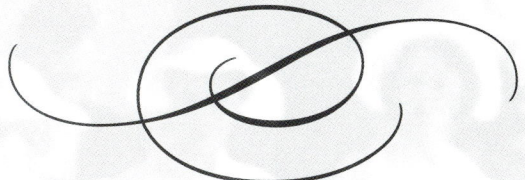

1950s

15 MAY 1953

Princess Ragnhild of Norway married
Erling Lorentzen.

19 APRIL 1956

Sovereign Prince Rainier III of Monaco
married American actress Grace Patricia Kelly.

2 JULY 1959

Prince Albert of Belgium married the
Italian Princess Paola Ruffo of Calabria.

19 April 1956, Monaco – Sovereign Prince Rainier III of Monaco married American actress Grace Patricia Kelly in civil and religious ceremonies which were televised around the world.

"The roar of the Metro-Goldwyn-Mayer lion has been echoing so loudly and unceasingly among the cliffs and crags of the Côte d'Azur lately

that the actual civil marriage of Prince Rainier of Monaco and Miss Grace Kelly, the film actress, was bound to run the risk of anti-climax. After such a great buildup, there could hardly but be a let down.

For there could not be anything of high romance, as Hollywood understands the phrase, in the bleak legal ceremony that took place in the throne room of the Palace of Monaco this morning. It was all legal formality and protocol, with no provision even for the exchange of a kiss between the principals – a fact that profoundly dismayed the journalists of the Western world who, though not meek, have managed to inherit for a little time all this Riviera world of bored or desperate pleasure."

From the *Times*, 19 April 1956

"… she was a figure of quite exceptional loveliness."

"Miss Kelly, whose air of controlled and icy composure could not at all conceal what might be called her stage fright, did not once smile either. She darted many a quick nervous glance at Prince Rainier, seated on her right, but apparently could not manage to catch his eye and draw any courage from that quarter. By all accounts, she was a figure of quite exceptional loveliness. She wore, they say, a severely simple dress of beige lace with a Peter Pan collar, and for most of the time kept her gloved hands very still in her lap. Her close-fitting hat revealed the artful simplicity of her hair style."

From the *Times,* 19 April 1956

6 May 1960

Princess Margaret of the United Kingdom
married Antony Armstrong-Jones.

12 January 1961

Princess Astrid of Norway married
Johan Martin Ferner.

25 & 30 May 1961

Princess Birgitta of Sweden married
Prince Johann Georg of Hohenzollern.

14 May 1962

Prince Juan Carlos of Spain married
Princess Sofía of Greece.

29 April 1964

Princess Irene of the Netherlands married
Carlist Prince Carlos of Bourbon-Parma.

5 June 1964

Princess Désirée of Sweden married
Baron Niclas Silfverschiöld.

30 June 1964

Princess Margaretha of Sweden married
London businessman John Ambler.

18 September 1964

Princess Anne-Marie of Denmark married
King Constantine II of Greece.

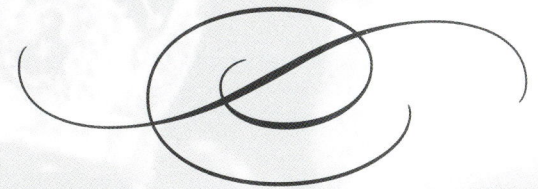

1960s

10 MARCH 1966

Princess Beatrix of the Netherlands married German diplomat Claus von Amsberg.

10 JANUARY 1967

Princess Margriet of the Netherlands married Pieter van Vollenhoven.

10 JUNE 1967

Princess Margrethe, Heir Apparent of Denmark, married Count Henri André of Laborde de Monpezat.

3 FEBRUARY 1968

Princess Benedikte of Denmark married Prince Richard zu Sayn-Wittgenstein-Berleburg.

29 AUGUST 1968

Crown Prince Harald of Norway married Sonja Haraldsen.

6 May 1960, United Kingdom – Princess Margaret of the United Kingdom married Antony Armstrong-Jones at Westminister Abbey, London (pictured left on the announcement of their engagement).

"From babyhood she had been the darling of a nation,
so adored and clucked over that it could fairly be said
50 million Britons looked upon Margaret Rose as a daughter.

Her joys and her occasional sadnesses were the people's as well. So intensely familiar was their interest that they felt free to offer her advice on the inclination of her heart. Four years ago they grieved when the laws of the Church of England backed by the stiff traditions of the Crown, forced her to forswear Group Caption Peter Townsend because he had been divorced. Lately, like a caucus of fidgety parents, they had openly fretted because their princess was approaching 30 and spinsterhood.

Now, after a well-concealed courtship and a brief engagement, Queen Elizabeth's only sister was getting married. The doting millions were electrified and delighted – and more than a little concerned. For in many ways this was a wildly unconventional union. Princess Margaret had elected to marry a commoner, the first such choice by British royalty in 450 years."

From *LIFE*, 16 May 1960

14 May 1962, Greece – Prince Juan Carlos of Spain (King Juan Carlos from 1975–present), married Princess Sofía of Greece in two successive ceremonies, at the Roman Catholic Church of St Denis and at the Greek Orthodox Cathedral of Athens.

"Once upon a time, a blue-eyed Princess of Greece was married to a six-foot, blond, curly haired Spanish Prince.

The Princess' wedding dress was all shimmering white with a frothy twenty-foot train carried by eight princesses from six countries, and everyone agreed that the Princess was as lovely as a swan.

Kings and queens, dukes and duchesses and counts and countesses came from all over Europe with gifts of sapphires and emeralds, rubies and pearls and other lovely things and hundreds of thousands of loyal subjects cheered in the streets…

… This fairy story happened here today to the real-life Princess Sophie of the Hellenes and Prince Juan Carlos."

From the *New York Times*, 15 May 1962

PRINCE JUAN CARLOS • PRINCESS SOFÍA

29 April 1964, Italy – Princess Irene of the Netherlands married Carlist Prince Carlos of Bourbon-Parma in Rome amid controversy.

"Princess Irene of the Netherlands, returned to Paris today after a weekend in the country to make preparations for her wedding in Rome to Don Carlos of Bourbon-Parma.

In an interview she gave to a Reuter correspondent today she said she was 'happy because love is wonderful, and unhappy because of the strain my family is going through'.

Don Carlos, who was by her side, said the Princess drew great comfort from daily telephone calls to Queen Juliana and Prince Bernhard, her parents (who have announced that they will not attend the wedding).

He added that 'certain political circles' had tried everything to prevent the marriage. 'This has been extremely painful both for Princess Irene and for her parents. It is cruel and unfair.'

He said that when political tension over the wedding had subsided, they planned to visit Holland. It would be Princess Irene's greatest joy to see her family again..."

From the *Times*, 21 April 1964

18 September 1964, Greece – Princess Anne-Marie of Denmark married King Constantine II of Greece at Athens.

"It was the first marriage of a reigning king of Greece in 100 years, and Athens made a memorable uproar."

"King Constantine of the Hellenes, the world's youngest monarch, married 18-year-old Princess Anne-Marie of Denmark this morning before a spectacular assemblage of royalty.

After a day of dazzling ceremony, the 24-year-old King and his bride flew off across the Aegean Sea on their wedding trip.

It was the first marriage of a reigning king of Greece in 100 years, and Athens made a memorable uproar. By 6 a.m. streets were crowded with swirls of people, estimated at nearly a million, waiting to see the procession to and from the cathedral. Every balcony in the city seemed to overflow with perspiring spectators, tossing strips of paper in red and blue, dominant colours in the flags of Denmark and Greece…

… The King wore the gleaming white uniform of a field marshal, it's high-crowned kepi accentuating his beaming boyish face. His tunic gleamed as the hot morning sunlight struck gold braid, ribbon, stars and badges of the four royal orders of Greece. The epaulettes bore the Greek letter 'P' in memory of his father, King Paul, who died last March.

'How I wish my dear father were with us today,' the King said at one point…

… Queen Ingrid, who wore a brilliant green dress and hat, watched the wedding of her youngest daughter with a worried but tender expression. It was apparent that Anne-Marie was nervous and that the heat affected her as much as it did many of the royal guests, who fanned themselves briskly during the ceremony. Except when Constantine smiled or whispered to her, she seemed transfixed."

From the *New York Times*, 18 September 1964

10 March 1966, the Netherlands – Princess Beatrix of the Netherlands (Queen Beatrix from 1980–present) married German diplomat Claus von Amsberg, despite protests.

14 November 1973

Princess Anne of the United Kingdom
married Captain Mark Phillips.

15 June 1974

Princess Christina of Sweden married
businessman Tord Magnuson.

1970s

28 JUNE 1975

Princess Christina of the
Netherlands married Cuban-born
New Yorker Jorge Guillermo.

19 JUNE 1976

King Carl XVI Gustaf of Sweden married
Silvia Renate Sommerlath.

28 JUNE 1978

Princess Caroline of Monaco married
businessman Philippe Junot.

14 November 1973, England – Princess Anne of the United Kingdom married Captain Mark Phillips at Westminster Abbey, London (pictured right, before their wedding).

"Yesterday the Dean of Westminster, the Very Rev Eric Abbot,
described the wedding ceremony for about 200 foreign journalists…

… he gratified them all by saying that Captain Phillips would be
wearing full army uniform with spurs and sword,
'and will look a very fine figure indeed'."

From the *Times*, 14 November 1973

19 June 1976, Sweden – King Carl XVI Gustaf of Sweden married Silvia Renate Sommerlath at Storkyrkan 'The Great Church' Cathedral, Stockholm.

"'When I first saw her it said "click"
and it has kept clicking since,' the 30-year old
king said recently at a news conference."

"The king and the commoner who clicked on their first meeting but kept their courtship secret for two years will marry in ceremonial splendor today, watched by European royalty and millions of television viewers.

King Carl XVI Gustaf and Silvia Sommerlath, daughter of a retired West German businessman, will be married in Storkyrkan Cathedral in the first wedding of a reigning Swedish monarch in 180 years…

… 'When I first saw her it said "click" and it has kept clicking since,' the 30-year old king said recently at a news conference.

The curly-haired monarch met his future bride at a private party during the 1972 summer Olympic games in Munich, where Miss Sommerlath was chief hostess. He had developed a reputation as a playboy, fond of fast cars, speedboats and discothèque dancing with a variety of girlfriends. But those days soon ended."

From the *Times-News*, 19 June 1976

28 June 1978, Monaco – Princess Caroline of Monaco married businessman Philippe Junot in civil and religious ceremonies.

"Princess Caroline of Monaco, the eldest daughter
of Prince Rainier and Princess Grace, has become engaged
to M Philippe Junot, a Paris insurance broker, it was officially
announced from the palace in Monte Carlo today…

… The announcement cuts short a spate of rumours about the imminent engagement of one of the most attractive heiresses in Europe.

For some years, Princess Caroline, who is just turned 20, has been regularly in the news. Her name, charm, vivacious personality and her real or supposed suitors have made the headlines of all the popular magazines and fed the gossip of society columns in this country and abroad.

Pop singers, American millionaires and the Prince of Wales have all, in turn, been mentioned as contenders for her hand. Every detail of her sentimental life and the social occasions attended by her were minutely reported, and the stories set many young and not-so-young French hearts throbbing.

She had become for millions a shining symbol of glamour and romance, with a touch of the fairy princess about her."

From the *Times*, 25 August 1977

29 JULY 1981
Prince Charles of the United Kingdom
married Lady Diana Spencer.

1980s

29 December 1983

Princess Caroline of Monaco married Stefano Casiraghi.

22 September 1984

Princess Astrid of Belgium married Arch-Duke Lorenz d'Autriche-Este.

23 July 1986

Prince Andrew of the United Kingdom married Sarah Ferguson.

29 July 1981, England – Prince Charles of the United Kingdom married Lady Diana Spencer at St Paul's Cathedral, London (pictured left on the announcement of their engagement).

> "In a break with royal precedent, Lady Diana Spencer has decided that she will not promise, at her wedding four weeks from today, to obey Prince Charles.

Queen Elizabeth II, Princess Margaret, Princess Anne and a long line of royal brides before them have included the word 'obey' in their wedding vows, as prescribed in the Anglican Book of Common Prayer dating from 1662.

But Lady Diana has chosen to follow the new ritual of the Church of England, and she will promise in the ceremony at St Paul's Cathedral only to 'love him, comfort him, honour and keep him, in sickness and in health'.

Prince Charles and his fiancée, both believers in a slow but steady evolution of royal tradition, were said to have held 'very serious' discussions on the point with the Archbishop of Canterbury, Dr Robert Runcie, before deciding to do what most modern English couples do."

From the *New York Times*, 2 July 1981

"The scale of Lady Diana's train, of a 25-foot length scarcely seen in an English church before, only became clear when she stepped out of her landau at St Paul's.

It was so long that its compression inside the coach had made creases which had to be straightened before she began the long walk to the altar. Later, as she moved to sign the register without bridesmaids to hold the train, it followed her like an elegant centipede.

After she had joined Charles, the couple managed to look directly ahead until the opening of the solemnisation of their matrimony came to the words 'it was ordained that children might be brought up…' then she flashed a sideways smile at him.

He, caught unawares, could not resist smiling back. And the smile began to turn into a laugh…

… But, throughout the rest of the service he dared looks at her, doing so with special emphasis on his vow to love and cherish."

From the *Guardian*, 30 July 1981

"Thousands of spectators jostled and joked in the
hot sunshine yesterday as they selected their vantage
points along the royal wedding route.

The West End of London was like the venue
for the world's greatest football match except
that everyone was supporting the same side.

'Wedding fever, wedding fever,' sang one hot
dog salesman in Piccadilly suddenly caught up
in a frenzy of unbridled patriots.

Outside Buckingham Palace the scene
resembled a giant picnic or pop festival
without the music. Many people had camped
during the night and most of them said they
had had little sleep."

From the *Guardian*, 29 July 1981

.... PRINCE CHARLES • LADY DIANA SPENCER ....

23 July 1986, England – Prince Andrew of the United Kingdom married Sarah Ferguson at Westminster Abbey, London (pictured left on the announcement of their engagement).

12 December 1992
Anne, The Princess Royal, of the
United Kingdom married Commander
Timothy Laurence.

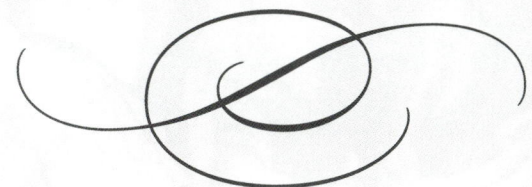

1990s

18 MARCH 1995

Infanta Elena of Spain married Jaime de Marichalar y Sáenz de Tejada.

1 JULY 1995

Princess Stephanie of Monaco married Daniel Ducruet.

18 NOVEMBER 1995

Prince Joachim of Denmark married Hong Kong-born Alexandra Christina Manley.

4 OCTOBER 1997

Infanta Cristina of Spain married Basque handball player Iñaki Urdangarín.

23 JANUARY 1999

Princess Caroline of Monaco married Prince Ernst of Hanover.

19 JUNE 1999

Prince Edward of the United Kingdom married Sophie Rhys-Jones.

4 DECEMBER 1999

Crown Prince Philippe of Belgium married Mathilde d'Udekem d'Acoz.

19 June 1999, United Kingdom – Prince Edward of the United Kingdom married Sophie Rhys-Jones at Windsor Castle.

"On a perfect day to get married, Queen Elizabeth's youngest child, Prince Edward, wed Sophie Rhys-Jones in the simplest and most subdued royal wedding Britain has seen for decades.

The 35-year-old groom, who runs a film production firm, and his 34-year-old bride, a public relations executive, are both media savvy and media shy. They thus planned a ceremony and a setting – Windsor Castle, 15 miles down the Thames from central London – that would preserve as much privacy as possible for a wedding that was broadcast around the world. The newlyweds wouldn't even provide the traditional post-nuptial kiss for the cameramen.

It was a striking departure from the lavish public festivals that marked the weddings of Edward (Windsor)'s sister, Anne, and his brothers Charles and Andrew. All three of those marriages ended in highly publicised divorces, and Edward reportedly concluded that he might avoid ending his marriage in the same way as his siblings if he didn't begin it the same way."

From the *Washington Post,* 20 June 1999

4 December 1999, Belgium – Crown Prince Philippe of Belgium married Mathilde d'Udekem d'Acoz in two ceremonies, at the Brussels town hall and at the Cathedral of St Michael.

"Within one storybook season, little-known speech therapist Mathilde d'Udekem became a princess after a spectacular wedding Saturday to Crown Prince Philippe and is now in line to become the kingdom's first Belgium-born queen.

In Belgium's biggest royal bash in decades, the only thing to outshine the ceremony and many crowned heads attending was Mathilde – dressed in an eggshell gown of crepe and silk. She trailed a century-old five-yard train of Brussels lace, and was topped in a jewelled tiara.

'Mathilde! Mathilde!' shouted thousands of people on the cobblestone Grand Place after Philippe and his bride appeared on the balcony of the gothic city hall. When the crown prince spoke of his wedding vows, cheers drifted through the windows from the crowd below.

'The whole of Belgium fell for your charms,' said Brussels mayor Knight Francois-Xavier de Donnea, at the civil ceremony which, under Belgium law had to precede the religious service."

From the *Post and Courier,* 5 December 1999

17 & 19 MAY 2001

Prince Constantijn of the Netherlands married Laurentien Brinkhorst.

25 AUGUST 2001

Crown Prince Haakon of Norway married Mette-Marit Tjessem Høiby.

2 FEBRUARY 2002

Crown Prince Willem-Alexander of the Netherlands married Máxima Zorreguieta.

24 MAY 2002

Princess Märtha Louise of Norway married Ari Mikael Behn.

12 APRIL 2003

Prince Laurent of Belgium married Claire Coombs.

12 SEPTEMBER 2003

Princess Stephanie of Monaco married Portuguese circus performer Adans Lopez Peres.

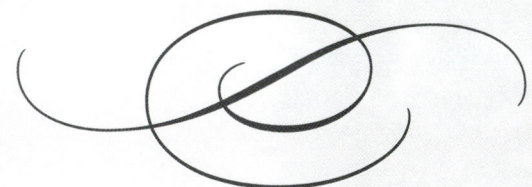

2000s

24 APRIL 2004

Prince Johan Friso of the Netherlands married Mabel Wisse Smit.

14 MAY 2004

Crown Prince Frederik of Denmark married Australian Mary Elizabeth Donaldson.

22 MAY 2004

Prince Felipe of Spain married former television presenter Letizia Ortiz.

9 APRIL 2005

Prince Charles of the United Kingdom married Camilla Parker Bowles.

24 MAY 2008

Prince Joachim of Denmark married Marie Agathe Odile Cavallier.

25 August 2001, Norway – Crown Prince Haakon of Norway married Mette-Marit Tjessem Høiby at Oslo Cathedral.

"With much of European royalty looking on,
the heir to the Norwegian throne, Crown Prince Haakon,
today exchanged marriage vows with a woman
who is no ordinary commoner.

She is Mette-Marit Tjessem Høiby, 28, a former waitress with a 4-year-old son from a previous relationship and an admitted history of heavy partying in Oslo's drug-filled 'house party' milieu. Barring the unexpected, she stands to become Norway's queen one day and one of Europe's most extraordinary sovereigns. For now, she is to be called Her Royal Majesty Crown Princess Mette-Marit, or more simply Mette-Marit…

… In a ceremony of pomp and splendor unusual for this egalitarian Nordic kingdom, Haakon and Mette-Marit were at their most majestic – she in a gown of white silk crepe, with a 20-foot-long veil, and he in black army uniform with red sash and medals. Yet all 800 people in the cathedral, including Prince Charles and several other future monarchs with troubles in love, knew that Haakon and Mette-Marit were staking out a liberating new way to be royal.

'In the last generation, they married commoners for the first time,' said Theo Aronson, an English biographer of monarchs. 'This younger generation is now breaking free.' Mette-Marit's rambunctious son, Marius, is hardly a liability. Already he has been dubbed Norway's 'charm troll' – a term of endearment – and he was front and center in the ceremony today."

From the *New York Times*, 26 August 2001

2 February 2002, the Netherlands – Crown Prince Willem-Alexander of the Netherlands married Máxima Zorreguieta in a civil ceremony at the Beurs van Berlage, Amsterdam, and a church ceremony at the Nieuwe Kerk, Amsterdam.

"When Queen Beatrix of the Netherlands watches her eldest son Willem-Alexander marry a glamorous Argentinian rancher's daughter, Máxima Zorreguieta, in Amsterdam today it will look like another fairy-tale royal wedding.

But behind all the pomp lurk tales of controversy which threatened at one point to stop the wedding taking place.

The main problem was that the bride's father – Jorge Zorreguieta – served as agriculture minister in the bloody Argentinian military dictatorship of Jorge Videla, which ruled from 1976 to 1983. Some 30,000 people were killed or disapeared under the regime.

Although Mr Zorreguieta is not accused of direct complicity in the crimes, it is alleged that he knew what was going on and did nothing to stop it. A Dutch government report reached the same conclusion but Máxima, 30, has said she believes her father's denials. Her husband-to-be, 34, has also chosen to give his controversial new father-in-law the benefit of the doubt...

… The credit for steering the royal family through these damaging episodes and keeping the wedding on track is all going to Máxima, a former New York investment banker.

She has wooed the Dutch public with a professionalism that may just have saved the monarchy and turned an embarassment into a public relations coup."

From the *Guardian,* 2 February 2002

14 May 2004, Denmark – Crown Prince Frederik of Denmark married Australian Mary Elizabeth Donaldson in a ceremony at Copenhagen Cathedral and reception at Fredensborg Castle.

"With a soundly delivered 'ja', the remarkable journey of Mary Elizabeth Donaldson from Australian commoner to European crown princess ended when she and her prince exchanged marriage vows in Copenhagen Cathedral last night.

Before 800 guests, including a who's who of Princess Mary's new regal relatives, an elegant Ms Donaldson, 32, pledged to love and honour Crown Prince Frederik, the 35-year-old heir to the Danish throne.

The love affair has captivated millions of Danes who talk of their 'Kaengu', kangaroo, in a tone bordering on reverence."

From the *Sydney Morning Herald*, 15 May 2004

CROWN PRINCE FREDERIK • MARY ELIZABETH DONALDSON

"I love you Mary. Come, let us go! Come, let us see!
Throughout a thousand worlds, weightless love awaits."

From wedding speech by Crown Prince Frederik to his bride

CROWN PRINCE FREDERIK • MARY ELIZABETH DONALDSON

9 April 2005, England – Prince Charles of the United Kingdom married Camilla Parker Bowles at the Guildhall in Windsor, followed by a service at St George's Chapel, Windsor Castle.

"They have overcome Becher's Brook and the Chair and all kinds of other terrible obstacles"

"Queen Elizabeth compared the long and finally consecrated love affair of her son and his bride to the running of the Grand National, in a speech following Prince Charles' wedding on Saturday that welcomed the new Duchess of Cornwall into the 'winner's enclosure' of the royal family.

The Queen opened her speech to the 800 assembled guests with an announcement that Hedgehunter, ridden by Ruby Walsh and trained by Willie Mullins, had won the historic race, before comparing the 34-year course

of Charles' and Camilla's relationship to the infamously difficult terrain of the Aintree steeplechase track.

'They have overcome Becher's Brook and the Chair and all kinds of other terrible obstacles,' the queen told the gathering of international crowned heads, literary and artistic luminaries, family and old friends of the couple. 'They have come through and I'm very proud and wish them well. My son is home and dry with the woman he loves. '"

From the *Irish Times*, 11 April 2005

PRINCE CHARLES • CAMILLA PARKER BOWLES

2010s

19 June 2010

Crown Princess Victoria of Sweden married
Daniel Westling.

19 June 2010, Sweden – Crown Princess Victoria of Sweden married Daniel Westling at Stockholm Cathedral.

PART TWO

WILLIAM & CATHERINE

WILLIAM &

9 January 1982

Catherine Elizabeth Middleton is born in England at the Royal Berkshire Hospital, Reading. She is the first child of Michael and Carole Middleton of Bradfield Southend, West Berkshire.

. . . .

20 June 1982

Catherine is christened in the church of St Andrew's Bradfield, in West Berkshire.

. . . .

21 June 1982

Prince William is born in England at St Mary's Hospital, Paddington, London. He weighs 7 pounds, 1½ ounces.

. . . .

4 August 1982

The Prince is christened William Arthur Philip Louis by the Archbishop of Canterbury, Dr Robert Runcie, in a ceremony at Buckingham Palace, London.

24 September 1985

Three-year-old Prince William starts at Mrs Mynor's Nursery School in West London.

15 January 1987

Prince William becomes a pupil at Wetherby Pre-preparatory School in Notting Hill, West London.

3 June 1991

Prince William is hit on the side of the head with a golf club while practising with a friend. He undergoes an operation for a depressed fracture of the forehead.

7 September 1995

Prince William begins his secondary education at Eton College in Windsor.

31 August 1997

Prince William's mother, Diana, Princess of Wales, is killed in a car crash in Paris.

. . . .

6 September 1997

Princes William and Harry walk behind their mother's funeral cortège and attend her funeral at Westminster Abbey.

1982 — 1984 — 1985 — 1986 — 1987 — 1990 — 1991 — 1992 — 1995 — 1996 — 1997 —

May 1984

The Middleton family moves to Amman, Jordan, where Catherine attends an English-language nursery school.

September 1986

The Middleton family returns to Berkshire, and Catherine becomes a pupil at St Andrew's School, near Pangbourne.

10 September 1990

Prince William starts at Ludgrove, an all-boys preparatory school in rural Berkshire.

December 1992

The official announcement of the separation of Prince William's parents, Prince Charles and Princess Diana, is made.

April 1996

Catherine becomes a pupil at Marlborough College, a coeducational boarding school in Wiltshire.

CATHERINE

11 April 2008

Prince William receives his RAF wings at RAF Cranwell having passed a challenging 12-week flying course. Catherine attends the ceremony.

....

17 May 2008

Catherine attends the marriage of Princess Anne's son Peter Phillips to Autumn Kelly and meets the Queen for the first time.

....

16 June 2008

The Queen officially appoints Prince William as the 1,000th Royal Knight Companion of the Most Noble Order of the Garter. Catherine attends the service.

26 March 2002

Prince William attends a charity fashion show in which his future bride Catherine is a model and comes to the public's attention for the first time.

....

September 2002

Prince William and Catherine move into a shared flat in St Andrews with two other students and later begin dating.

April 2004

Prince William and Catherine are photographed together for the first time on a Royal skiing holiday in Klosters, Switzerland.

2006

Following her graduation, Catherine begins work for Party Pieces, a company owned by her family, and also works part-time for Jigsaw Junior.

....

15 December 2006

Prince William graduates from the Royal Military Academy Sandhurst. He is commissioned as an army officer and joins the Blues and Royals of the Household Cavalry as a Second Lieutenant.

25 February 2011

Prince William and Catherine launch the 600th anniversary celebrations at the University of St Andrews.

....

29 April 2011

Prince William marries Catherine in Westminster Abbey, London.

2001 — 2002 — 2003 — 2004 — 2005 — 2006 — 2007 — 2008 — 2010 — 2011

July 2000–August 2001

William and Catherine both undertake gap years. Prince William visits Chile, Belize and Africa and works on British dairy farms. Catherine studies in Florence, Italy, participates in a development programme in Chile and crews on Round the World Challenge boats in Solent, England.

....

September 2001

Prince William and Catherine meet at the University of St Andrews in Fife, Scotland, where they both begin their undergraduate studies. They both have rooms in St Salvators Hall of Residence.

21 June 2003

Prince William celebrates his 21st birthday with an African-themed party at Windsor Castle. Catherine is a guest.

23 June 2005

Prince William and Catherine graduate from the University of St Andrews, Scotland. He is awarded a 2:1 Master of Arts (Honours) in Geography, and she a 2:1 in History of Art.

....

October 2005

Prince William passes the Regular Commission Board assessments and is accepted to the Royal Military Academy Sandhurst.

....

September 2005

Prince William takes on his first patronage, for homeless charity Centrepoint.

9 January 2007

A media frenzy occurs outside Catherine's home on her 25th birthday. Prince William later requests she be left alone.

....

14 April 2007

A split in the relationship between Prince William and Catherine is confirmed.

....

1 July 2007

Prince William and his brother Prince Harry host the Concert for Diana which Catherine also attends. Their relationship is rekindled.

16 November 2010

The Prince of Wales announces that Prince William and Catherine have become engaged in October 2010 while on holiday in Kenya. They give their first interview as an engaged couple.

COURTSHIP

In the autumn of September 2001, as the leaves began to fall, Prince William and Catherine Middleton enrolled at the University of St Andrews and a love affair began.

Prince William claims to have recognised something special in Catherine from their first meeting in 2001. At the time, they were both new undergraduate students at the University of St Andrews in Scotland, and both had been assigned to St Salvators Hall of Residence. Initially, Catherine felt more at home at St Andrews than did Prince William – to avoid excessive media interest, Prince William had missed Freshers' Week, a time when many events take place to help new students settle in.

Catherine remembers her first introduction to the prince, recalling that her face reddened and that she scurried away shyly.

Her initial discomfort, however, soon passed and the two quickly developed a relaxed and easy manner with one another. They were close friends for more than a year before their romance began. They would help one another with assignments and soon came to realise that they shared many interests and a sense of humour, often gently teasing one another.

For their second year at university, Prince William, Catherine and two other students moved into a shared flat in St Andrews town and it was here that the couple's romance slowly began to blossom.

Above: Catherine at the Wimbledon Lawn Tennis Championships in London. Right: Prince William arriving for his first day at the University of St Andrews.

Prince William believes that they created a
firm foundation for their marriage by establishing a
friendship before a romantic relationship.

Above, left: Prince William, Catherine and Pippa Middleton after a Field Game match at Eton College, Eton. Above, right: Prince William and Catherine on a skiing holiday in Klosters.

The public first learned of Prince William and Catherine's relationship in 2004 when they were photographed together while on holiday at Klosters, a Swiss ski resort.

Since then, the couple has remained close. While they did break their relationship for several months in 2007, they were still seen together on occasion and were photographed near each other at the Concert for Diana, held ten years after the Princess of Wales' death. The couple was soon back together and Catherine continued to attend events with Prince William.

Above, top: Prince Harry, Prince William and Catherine at a Six Nations Championship rugby match at Twickenham, London.
Above: Prince Harry, Prince William and Catherine at the Concert for Diana, Wembley, London.

Left and above: Prince William, his grandmother Queen Elizabeth II and Catherine during the Sovereign's Parade at the Royal Military Academy Sandhurst, Surrey, England.

In 2006, Catherine attended Prince William's graduation from the Royal Military Academy Sandhurst.

Catherine's first official Royal public occasion was in 2008 when she attended Prince William's Order of the Garter ceremony at Windsor Castle. After the announcement of their engagement on 16 November 2010, Prince William and Catherine gave a television interview where they appeared to be deeply in love, and attributed the strength of their relationship to its developing over many years of living together, having many interests in common and a shared sense of humour.

In February 2011, they appeared together once again when they launched the 600th anniversary celebrations of the University of St Andrews, bringing them back to the place where their courtship first began.

Above: Prince William and Catherine after his graduation as a Royal Air Force (RAF) pilot at Royal Air Force Cranwell, Lincolnshire.
Right: Catherine at the wedding of Laura Parker Bowles and Harry Lopes, at St Cyriac's Church, Lacock, Wiltshire.

PROPOSAL &
ENGAGEMENT

Although Catherine and Prince William
had discussed the possibility of marriage, his actual
proposal came as a surprise to Catherine.

The two were holidaying in a cottage in Kenya, Africa, with a group of friends at the time. Prince William had planned every detail long in advance to ensure that everything went well. Although what actually transpired remains a secret, Catherine has revealed that it was extremely romantic and that, of course, she accepted.

Left: Prince William and Catherine announce their engagement, St James's Palace, London, England, 16 November 2010.

Above and opposite: Prince William and Catherine at their first public appearance since announcing their engagement, at the Naming Ceremony and Service of Dedication for the Atlantic 85 Lifeboat 'Hereford Endeavour' in Anglesey, North Wales.

Prince William and Catherine attribute the strength of their relationship to its developing over many years of living together, having many interests in common and a shared sense of humour.

Above: Prince William and Catherine during a visit to the University of St Andrews to mark the start of its 600th anniversary.
Right: Catherine and Prince William attend Harry Meade and Rosie Bradford's wedding at the Church of St Peter and St Paul, Northleach near Cheltenham.

Prince William ensured that his mother was a part of the occasion by presenting Catherine with Princess Diana's own sapphire-and-diamond engagement ring.

Prince William had been carrying the ring in his rucksack for about three weeks, not letting it out of his sight. William followed tradition by asking Catherine's father for permission to marry his daughter. However, he did not do so until after proposing to Catherine. He admitted that he was too worried that Michael Middleton might refuse. As it turned out, both Catherine's parents and his own father were thrilled with the news.

While the proposal took place in October 2010, it was not until 16 November that Prince Charles, the Prince of Wales, officially announced the engagement. On 23 November 2010, Jamie Lowther-Pinkerton, Private Secretary to Prince William and Prince Harry, announced that the wedding would take place at Westminster Abbey on 29 April 2011, a date chosen because it is the feast day of Saint Catherine.

Right: 16 November 2010, England – a close-up of Catherine's engagement ring, St James's Palace, London.

WEDDING

On 29 April 2011, Prince William and Catherine Middleton were married at Westminster Abbey.

London was decorated in style for the wedding. A multitude of Union Jacks lined The Mall and flew outside Westminster Abbey as well as on many other buildings around the city.

Two giant media stands were erected, one outside Buckingham Palace and the other outside Westminster Abbey, and between them they commanded spectacular views of the church doors and of the balcony at Buckingham Palace.

The threat of rain did not stop thousands of people, including many foreign visitors, from lining the route of the Royal procession the day before the wedding.

Left: David and Victoria Beckham arrive at Westminster Abbey. Above: Guests including Sir Elton John in Westminster Abbey.

Prince William and Catherine invited nearly 2,000 guests to the service at Westminster Abbey.

As well as members of the British Royal Family and of Catherine's family, the guest list included members of foreign royal families, dignitaries and members of governments, parliaments and devolved administrations from around the world, senior members of the defence services, religious leaders, representatives of charities supported by Prince William and also many individuals chosen by Prince William or Catherine because of personal connections. This last group included people associated with the armed services, entertainment and sport and, of course, close friends. Of those invited to the service, about 600 went on to the reception at Buckingham Palace and about 300 were also invited to dinner and dancing afterwards.

Santa Palmer-Tomkinson and Tara Palmer-Tomkinson arrive at Westminster Abbey.

Arriving at the West Door of Westminster Abbey (clockwise from top): Charlene Wittstock, the fiancée of Prince Albert II of Monaco; Princesses Eugenie and Beatrice of York; Sophie, Countess of Wessex and Anne, The Princess Royal.

Left and above: Carole Middleton, Prince Charles and Camilla, Duchess of Cornwall arrive at Westminster Abbey.

Prime Minister of the United Kingdom, David Cameron.

Above: Earl Spencer's daughters, Lady Kitty (front) and Lady Amelia, in Westminster Abbey. Overleaf: The Very Reverend Dr John Hall, Dean of Westminster, greets Queen Elizabeth II.

Previous page: Prince William arrives at Westminster Abbey. Left and above: Prince William and Prince Harry.

Few were surprised when Prince William chose his younger brother Harry to be his best man.

Like the Middleton sisters, Princes William and Harry went to the same schools and grew up to become close friends and confidants.

At the wedding, Prince William wore his red Colonel of the Irish Guards dress uniform with his blue Order of the Garter sash and star and his RAF wings. In contrast, Prince Harry wore his black Captain of the Household Cavalry uniform with his Golden Jubilee and Afghanistan campaign medals.

Above and overleaf: Catherine arrives at Westminster Abbey in the Queen's Rolls Royce Phantom VI.

Tom Pettifer laughs as he arrives at Westminster Abbey with William Lowther-Pinkerton, Lady Louise Windsor and The Honourable Margarita Armstrong-Jones.

Maid of Honour Philippa Middleton arrives with Bridesmaids Grace van Cutsem and Eliza Lopes.

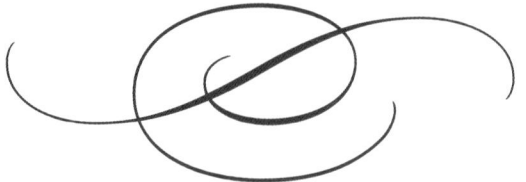

Catherine wore a wedding dress styled by British designer Sarah Burton, the creative director of British fashion house, Alexander McQueen.

Inspired by Grace Kelly's bridal gown of 1956, the dress was a breathtakingly beautiful medieval-style strapless dress made of ivory and white satin gazar, a loosely woven silk, covered by a long-sleeved lace bodice and finished with a 2.7 metre train. The bodice drew on the Victorian tradition of corsetry and is a hallmark of McQueen design.

The lace was handcrafted by the Royal School of Needlework at Hampton Court Palace and incorporated embroidery representing emblems of the four countries of the United Kingdom: the rose of England, thistle of Scotland, daffodil of Wales and shamrock of Ireland. In keeping with the theme of nature, the full skirt was intended to resemble an opening flower.

As Catherine arrived at Westminster Abbey, her face was covered by a light silk tulle veil held in place with a Cartier 'halo' tiara made in 1936 and loaned to her by Queen Elizabeth for the occasion. Catherine's earrings, made by Robinson Pelham, were pear-shaped diamond drops with a pave-set diamond acorn suspended in the middle of each one. They were a gift from Catherine's parents and reflected the acorns in her coat of arms.

Catherine's shoes were also from Alexander McQueen, and were made of ivory duchesse satin and lace embroidered by the Royal School of Needlework.

Catherine's bouquet included myrtle, sweet william, hyacinth and lily of the valley.

Catherine enters Westminster Abbey along with her father Michael Middleton and sister Philippa.

Breaking with tradition, Philippa Middleton, the Maid of Honour, also wore white.

Her long, form-fitting dress had a cowl neck and cap sleeves, and was made of ivory satin-based crepe with fifty-eight gazar-and-organza-covered buttons. Like the bridal gown, it was created by 36-year-old British designer Sarah Burton for Alexander McQueen.

Known to her friends and family as Pippa or simply Pip, Philippa is little more than a year and a half younger than is Catherine and the two have a close friendship. They have followed similar paths in life, attending the same schools and each studying at university in Scotland.

Catherine and her father walk down the aisle.

Michael Middleton and Catherine join Prince William at the entrance to the High Altar of Westminster Abbey.

The choice of Westminster Abbey for the marriage service was intensely meaningful for Prince William and the entire Royal Family.

It was the site of many other royal weddings and of Prince William's mother's funeral service, which he attended at the age of fifteen. The couple admired the Abbey for its staggering beauty, as well as its history and because it can hold at least 2,000 people whilst retaining an intimate atmosphere at the High Altar.

Above and right: Prince William gives Catherine a ring made from a nugget of Welsh gold gifted to him by the Queen shortly after the couple's engagement.
Overleaf: Prince William and Catherine in the Sacrarium.

"I, William Arthur Philip Louis, take thee
Catherine Elizabeth to my wedded wife to have
and to hold from this day forward.

For better, for worse. For richer, for poorer.
In sickness and in health.

To love and to cherish. Till death us do part.
According to God's holy law. And thereto I give thee my troth."

THE KINGDOMS OF THIS WORLD ARE BECOME THE KINGDOMS

Mother of the Bride Carole Middleton and Catherine's brother James.

Queen Elizabeth II and Prince Philip, Duke of Edinburgh.

Prince William and Catherine, the Duke and Duchess of Cambridge.

After the ceremony: Prince Charles, Prince Philip, the Duchess of Cornwall and Queen Elizabeth II.

Above: Michael and Carole Middleton. Overleaf: The Duke and Duchess of Cambridge proceed to Buckingham Palace in the 1902 State Landau.

Prince Harry travels down The Mall with Lady Louise Windsor and Tom Pettifer in an Ascot Landau horse-drawn carriage.

Queen Elizabeth II and Prince Philip, Duke of Edinburgh ride in a Semi-State Landau to Buckingham Palace.

Philippa Middleton travels down The Mall to Buckingham Palace.

Previous and this page: The Duke and Duchess of Cambridge arrive at Buckingham Palace and greet Prime Ministers of Australia and New Zealand.

Previous and this page: Supporters fill The Mall as the Royal Family, the Middleton family, and the Wedding Party appear on the balcony of Buckingham Palace.

Michael and Carole Middleton, Eliza Lopes, Prince Charles, the Duchess of Cornwall, Lady Louise Windsor, Grace van Cutsem, the Duchess and Duke of Cambridge,

Hon. Margarita Armstrong-Jones, Tom Pettifer, William Lowther-Pinkerton, Queen Elizabeth II, Prince Philip, Philippa Middleton, Prince Harry and James Middleton.

Previous page: The Royal Air Force Battle of Britain Memorial Flight flies over Buckingham Palace.

Above and overleaf: The Duke and Duchess of Cambridge leave Buckingham Palace for Clarence House in Prince Charles' Aston Martin DB6.

God our Father, we thank you for our families,
for the love that we share and for the joy of our marriage.

In the busyness of each day keep our eyes fixed on what is
real and important in life and help us to be generous with
our time and love and energy.

Strengthened by our union, help us to
serve and comfort those who suffer.
We ask this in the Spirit of Jesus Christ.

Amen.

Prince William and Catherine's Wedding Prayer.

ISBN 978-1-74270-224-7

Produced and originated by PQ Blackwell Limited
116 Symonds Street, Auckland 1010, New Zealand
www.pqblackwell.com

Published in 2011 by Hardie Grant Books

Hardie Grant Books (Australia)
Ground Floor, Building 1
658 Church Street
Richmond, Victoria 3121
www.hardiegrant.com.au

Hardie Grant Books (UK)
Dudley House, North Suite
34–35 Southampton Street
London WC2E 7HF
www.hardiegrant.co.uk

Concept and design copyright © 2011 PQ Blackwell Limited
Book design by Sarah Anderson and Victoria Skinner
Edited by Lisette du Plessis
Additional text by Mary Atkinson, copyright © 2011 PQ Blackwell Limited

Printed by Everbest Printing Co Ltd, China

Image Credits

Images used with permission of Getty Images and the copyright holders except page 62: Terence Donovan Archive/Getty Images; and pages 194–195: Photograph by: SAC Neil Chapman; © UK MOD Crown copyright 2011.

Literary Permissions

The publisher is grateful for literary permissions to reproduce the quotations appearing in this book, subject to copyright. The publisher asserts that although quotations may be widely attributed to one author, it is not always possible to confirm the exact original source of a quotation. However, the publisher acknowledges that every effort has been made to trace the copyright holders, and apologises for any unintentional omission. We would be pleased to hear from any not acknowledged here and to undertake to make all reasonable efforts to include the appropriate acknowledgement in any subsequent editions.

Extracts from *The Times of London* on pages 23–24, 33, 42 and 50: Reprinted by permission of *The Times*/NI Syndication; Extract from *LIFE* on page 29: Copyright 1960 The Picture Collection Inc. Reprinted with permission. All rights reserved; Extracts from *The New York Times* as follows on page 30: from *The New York Times* 15 May 1962 © 1962; page 35: from *The New York Times* 18 September 1964 © 1964; page 55: from *the New York Times* 2 July 1981 © 1981; Page 75: from *the New York Times*, 26 August 2001 © 2001. All rights reserved. Used by permission and protected by the Copyright Laws of the United States. The printing, copying, redistribution, or retransmission of this Content without express written permission is prohibited; Extracts from *The Guardian* on page 47: Copyright Guardian News & Media Ltd 1947; page 58 and 61: Copyright Guardian News & Media Ltd 1981; and page 78: Copyright Guardian News & Media Ltd 2002; Extract from *The Washington Post* on page 67: © *The Washington Post*; Extract from *The Sydney Morning Herald* and *The Age* on page 81: © Peter Fray/*The Age*.